know your
POODLE

Earl Schneider, editor

THE PET LIBRARY LTD

THE PET LIBRARY LTD

The Pet Library Ltd, 50 Cooper Square, New York, N.Y. Exclusive Canadian Distributors: VioBin (Canada) Ltd.—Canadian Aquarium Supply Co., 1125 Talbot Street, St. Thomas, Ontario, Canada.

PRINTED IN THE NETHERLANDS

CONTENTS

1 The friendly aristocrat   page   3

2 Selecting your pet   page   8

3 The new puppy   page 13

4 Learning the obedience commands   page 23

5 Good grooming   page 27

6 General care   page 31

7 Common ailments   page 39

8 Poodle breeding   page 46

9 Scientific breeding   page 50

10 Grooming for the bench   page 51

11 Pals with the Poodle   page 59

1 The friendly aristocrat

The poodle is the attractive, lively Prince of Dogs. Whichever variety you choose, the Toy Poodle, the Miniature Poodle, or the Standard Poodle, you will have a pet who has won the hearts of dog lovers everywhere. Possessing incomparable style and a quick intelligence, he makes a loyal and aristocratic companion who will add joy to your household.

Scholars are still uncertain about the Poodle's origins, but it is a well-known fact that fifteenth-century European nobles considered him an excellent hunting dog. Through subsequent centuries his sterling qualities came to be appreciated all over the world. In recent years this intelligent breed has attained prominence in the demanding world of television and circus, and has been outstanding in obedience trials in the United States and England.

Since Poodles were used extensively for retrieving game from water, their heavy coats proved to be a hindrance. It became a common procedure to clip the legs and the rear half of the Poodle's coat leaving small tufts on the Poodle's joints and hocks. From a utilitarian practice, it soon became fashionable to clip Poodles in this style. Similarly, another fashion of tying up the "top knot" with a colorful ribbon, rose from the need to locate the Poodle as he retrieved game in the water. Clipping the Poodle quickly became popular throughout Europe. The French, a people noted for their interest in fashion, enthusiastically began to clip Poodles in exotic styles.

The two show clips, the Continental and the English Saddle, are descendants of the early French styles. Nowadays, "French" and "Poodles" are words that the public links together. And why not? Until recently, you could see barbers on the streets of Paris clipping Poodles in the most incredible styles.

Poodles love affection.

Standard of breed

The description and standards adopted by the Poodle Club of America and approved by the American Kennel Club, February 14, 1940 (amended in accordance with ruling of the American Kennel Club, July 14, 1943) follow:

Poodle

General appearance, carriage and condition: That of a very active, intelligent and elegant-looking dog, squarely built, well-proportioned, moving soundly and carrying himself proudly. Properly clipped in the traditional fashion and carefully groomed, the Poodle has about him an air of distinction and dignity peculiar to himself.

Silver Toy. The puppy clip is accepted by the American Kennel Club.

Head and expression: (a) *Skull:* moderately rounded, with a slight but definite stop. Cheek-bones and muscles flat. *Muzzle:* long, straight and fine, with slight chiseling under the eyes. Strong without lippiness. The chin definite enough to preclude snipiness. Teeth white, strong and with a scissors bite. Nose sharp with well-defined nostrils. (b) *Eyes:* set far apart, very dark, full of fire and intelligence, oval in appearance. (c) *Ears:* set low and hanging close to the head. The leather should be long, wide and heavily feathered.

Neck and shoulders: Neck well proportioned, strong and long to admit of the head being carried high and with dignity. Skin snug at throat. The neck should rise from strong muscular shoulders which slope back from their point of angulation at the upper foreleg to the withers.

Body: The chest deep and moderately wide. The ribs well sprung and braced up. The back short, strong and slightly hollowed, the loins short, broad and muscular. (Bitches may be slightly longer in back than dogs.)

Tail: Straight, set on rather high, docked, but of sufficient length to insure a balanced outline. It should be carried up and in a gay manner.

Legs: The forelegs straight from the shoulder, parallel and with bone and muscle in proportion to size of dog. The pasterns should be strong. The hind legs very muscular, stifles well bent and hocks well let down. The thigh should be well developed, muscular and showing width in the region of the stifle to insure strong and graceful action. The four feet should turn neither in nor out.

Feet: Rather small and oval in shape. Toes arched, close and cushioned on thick, hard pads.

Coat: Quality: very profuse, of harsh texture and dense throughout.

Clip: A Poodle may be shown in the "Puppy" Clip or in the traditional "Continental" Clip or the "English Saddle" Clip. A Poodle under a year old may be shown in the "Puppy" Clip with the coat long except the face, feet and base of tail, which should be shaved. Dogs one year old or older must be shown in either the "Continental" Clip or "English Saddle" Clip.

In the "Continental" Clip the hindquarters are shaved with pompons on hips (optional). The face, feet, legs and tail are shaved leaving bracelets on the hind legs, puffs on the forelegs and a pompon at the end of the tail. The rest of the body must be left in full coat.

In the "English Saddle" Clip the hindquarters are covered with a short blanket of hair except for a curved shaved area on the flank and two shaved bands on each hind leg. The face, feet, forelegs and tail are shaved leaving puffs on the forelegs and a pompon at the end of the tail. The rest of the body must be left in full coat.

Color: The coat must be an even and solid color at the skin. In blues, grays, silvers, browns, cafe-au-laits, apricots and creams the coats may show varying shades of the same color. This is frequently present in the somewhat darker feathering of the ears and in the tipping of the ruff. While clear colors are definitely preferred such natural variation in the shading of the coat is not to be considered a fault. Brown and cafe-au-lait Poodles have liver-colored noses, eye-rims and lips, dark toenails and dark amber eyes. Black, blue, gray, silver, apricot, cream and white Poodles have black noses, eye-rims and lips, black or self-colored toenails and very dark eyes. In the apricots while black is preferred, liver-colored noses, eye-rims and lips, self-colored toenails and amber eyes are permitted but are not desirable.

Gait: A straightforward trot with light springy action. Head and tail carried high. Forelegs and hind legs should move parallel turning neither in nor out. Sound movement is essential.

Size

Standard: The Standard Poodle is over 15 inches at the withers. Any Poodle which is 15 inches or less in height shall be disqualified from competition as a Standard Poodle.

Miniature: The Miniature Poodle is 15 inches or under at the withers, with a minimum height in excess of 10 inches. Any Poodle which is over 15 inches, or 10 inches or less at the withers shall be disqualified from competition as a Miniature Poodle.

Toy: The Toy Poodle is 10 inches or under at the withers. Any Poodle which is more than 10 inches at the withers shall be disqualified from competition as a Toy Poodle.

Major faults

Eyes: round in appearance, protruding, large or very light. Jaws: undershot, overshot or wry mouth. Cowhocks. Feet: flat or spread. Tail: set low, curled or carried over the back. Shyness.

Disqualifications

Parti-colors: The coat of a parti-colored dog is not an even solid color at the skin but is variegated in patches of two or more colors.
Any type of clip other than those listed in section on coat.
Any size over or under the limits specified in section on size.

Value of points

General appearance, carriage and condition	20
Heads, ears, eyes and expression	20
Neck and shoulders	10
Body and tail	15
Legs and feet	15
Coat—color and texture	10
Gait	10
Total	100

2 Selecting your pet

Among dog enthusiasts it is readily acknowledged that owning a Poodle is a tribute to one's recognition of what is best. In the home his lively personality soon makes him a cherished member of the family. His aristocratic and elegant appearance graces your home with beauty. His unrestrained affection, sprightly intelligence, and persevering loyalty is a combination of qualities rarely to be found in any other citizen of the canine kingdom. Whether Toy, Miniature, or Standard,

Poodles are fine companions for an outdoor ramble.

children easily fall in love with them; their natural clowning appeals to all.

Female and male Poodles differ slightly in temperament. Both are equally affectionate, but the male has a characteristic friskiness about him that many people like. Of course, if you like puppies or wish to breed Poodles, select a female. You will be able to feel like a proud grandparent and think of how happy your friends will be when you give them a cute Poodle puppy. Or, if you want to keep most of the puppies, it will be like having another family. Buy a good female, select the best stud available and you may even realize a profit on your breeding.

Registration papers

In most cases your puppy will be from a registered litter. This means that the litter has been officially recognized by the American Kennel Club and the parentage, as well as the number of puppies, is on file. Your Poodle must be registered in case you decide to enter him in a show someday. So, be sure to do this as soon as you get him. The pet shop owner from whom you have purchased the puppy will give you an application signed by the breeder and tell you how to fill it out.

As with a child, giving your Poodle a name will be a creative challenge. Poodles that we know have such varying names as Hoor, Teeschy, Drake, and Maintenon. Some Poodle owners show the pedigree in names; for example, the son of Drake can be called Drake II or Drake Jr. A good rule is to pick a name that suits your Poodle's personality.

After your Poodle's name has been registered ask your seller, or write to the American Kennel Club, for his pedigree. A pedigree traces his family tree. Why is this important to have? Well, if you decide to breed your Poodle a knowledge of his general ancestry is helpful. Identifying his parents, grandparents, and great-grandparents indicates the quality of his breeding.

Having registered him, named him, and obtained his pedigree, you now have a Poodle with the proper credentials for entering the show ring and obedience competitions.

His irresistible appeal

Some Poodle owners never had to choose their Poodle. A neighbor or close friend owned a Poodle who gave birth to a litter of lively pups. All that was necessary for these lucky people was to pick the one they liked best. But, if you are not so fortunate, you may find the right Poodle at a nearby kennel or pet shop. Your telephone book is the best place to find a list of kennels and pet shops specializing in Poodles. Similarly, dog magazines and your newspapers carry many useful advertisements.

Poodle puppies are so appealing that when you first see a litter the temptation to take one home may prove irresistible. Exercise careful judgement in selecting the puppy that is right for you. After looking at puppies in several pet shops or kennels, you will soon notice differences in temperament and appearance. Look for an active puppy, one that is bold, venturesome and full of mischief. In each litter there is one puppy who shows a zest for life and precociousness unequalled by his littermates.

Appearance is a good guide to a puppy's health. A puppy's eyes and ears should be clear. Check his teeth and gums. The upper teeth should project ever so slightly over the lower for a scissors bite. The gums should be a healthy pink. A firm, non-watery bowel movement is a sign of his good health. Normally it is wise to choose a young puppy; he will adapt to a new environment more quickly.

Most reputable pet shops and kennels allow you to take the puppy you have selected to a veterinarian for a general check up. Since the veterinarian will be one of your dog's best friends, his approval of your purchase is essential. If the veterinarian disapproves of your choice you will usually have the option of getting either a refund or another puppy.

Now watch the little birdie!

3   The new puppy

Your puppy should have a special place of his own. It can be anywhere, under a table, next to your bed, or beside a chair. His bed should be put away from drafts and dampness, preferably in a dark corner and large enough for him to curl up in. The bed can be a shallow cardboard box, a regular dog basket, or a bed purchased at your pet shop.

Other things your puppy needs are two dishes, one for food and one for liquids. Make sure his toys are solid and hard.

Along with his bed, dishes, and toys, you will need a comb and brush. A strong steel comb with fine teeth at one end and

A puppy likes a bed of his own.

SALLY ANNE THOMPSON

medium teeth at the other will suffice. You will also need a stiff long wire-bristled brush (for Toy Poodles use the small size with rounded teeth.) Ask your pet supply dealer for information concerning types of collars, leashes and accessories which are especially suited to your Poodle.

With proper care and understanding your puppy's first night away from his mother, brothers and sisters should not be trying. In his new surroundings what he needs most is security. The "tick-tock" of a towel-wrapped clock in his bed will lessen any loneliness he may feel; a cloth doll will give him something warm to nestle to.

If you provide all possible comfort for him on his first night he will quickly grow to love his new home. Should he cry don't make the mistake of picking him up or petting him. He will then cry every time he wants to be petted. Show him from the beginning that crying will only result in stern disapproval.

Fuel for growth

Because your puppy's food is the fuel for his growth, you will want to plan a balanced diet for him. When you get a new pup, find out from his previous owner his feeding schedule and the type of food he has been getting. Like a child's, his stomach is sensitive to a sudden change in diet, so introduce any new food gradually, by adding small amounts of it to the food he's accustomed to. Gradually increase the amount of the new item while reducing the old until the changeover is complete.

Meat, boiled milk, or cottage cheese are essential to the diet of a young puppy. A nourishing grade of meal or kibble is an important part of the older pup's diet. Remember that the Standard and Miniature are much larger dogs than the Toy, and they can be fed food that should not be given to the Toy until he's five or six months old.

Your puppy is full of life and needs plenty of food to keep him active. Feed him four times daily, in the morning, noon, early evening, and night. After several months, he will begin to eye scraps of food on your table. Why don't you give him a tidbit? But NOT from the table. After you've finished your meal put it in his own dish, in its usual spot. Otherwise you'll have a beggar at the table and this can become a nuisance. He will also begin to like cooked horse meat, canned dog food, and dry dog food moistened with milk, water or broth.

When your puppy is three months old you may begin to reduce the number of his daily meals. At this age, he is satisfied with three meals. But if he still wants another meal, don't refuse it. At six months reduce the feedings to twice daily. Within a few months, at one year old, he will be eating one meal a day and then you will know that your puppy has grown up! Toy Poodles, because of their small size, sometimes find it difficult to maintain adequate body reserves. Extra meals, particularly during the critical first six months, are very beneficial.

Chef's choice

Picking the right dog food is a problem for all dog owners. You have seen many brands of dog biscuits selling at different prices. Some of the biscuits are made from manufacturer's by-products. Others are top grade wheat bought solely to be used as flour in dog biscuits.

Check the amount of protein a brand of dog food contains before you buy it. The package that has the highest percentage of protein for the money is always the best buy. It is always best to buy your Poodle food with a high protein content.

Carbohydrates, fats, vitamins and minerals also play an important role in your Poodle's diet. Dog biscuits are a good source of carbohydrates. Fats are obtained from lard, lamb, fish, chicken, suet, vegetable oils, and bacon fat. Reputable manufacturers of dog food make sure their products contain all the vitamins your Poodle needs. If your Poodle has a balanced diet his mineral needs will also be well taken care of.

Poodles love to play.

Poodles are natural retrievers.

Reward him when he does well.

Age 2 Months

Morning: 1 to 3 tablespoonfuls milk; $\frac{1}{2}$ to $1\frac{1}{2}$ tablespoonfuls cereal.

Noon: 1 to 2 heaping teaspoonfuls raw ground meat.

Afternoon: Repeat morning feeding.

Evening: Repeat noon feeding.

Late evening: 1 to 3 tablespoonfuls milk; $\frac{1}{4}$ to $\frac{1}{2}$ teaspoonful cod-liver oil once a day.

Age 3 Months

Gradually increase amounts per feeding, according to puppy's growth and capacity. Gradually eliminate afternoon and late evening feeding.

Age 4 Months

Morning: 2 to 4 tablespoonfuls milk; 1 to 2 tablespoonfuls cereal.

Noon: 1 to 2 heaping tablespoonfuls raw meat.

Evening: 1 to 2 heaping tablespoonfuls raw meat; $\frac{1}{2}$ to 1 teaspoonful cooked, mashed vegetables.

$\frac{1}{2}$ to 1 teaspoonful cod-liver oil once a day.

Age 5 Months

Increase amount per feeding.

Age 6 Months

Morning: $\frac{1}{4}$ to $\frac{3}{4}$ cups milk; 2 to 6 tablespoonfuls cereal.

Noon: 1 to 3 heaping tablespoonfuls meat; 1 to 3 tablespoonfuls cereal.

Evening: $1\frac{1}{2}$ to 4 heaping tablespoonfuls meat; $1\frac{1}{2}$ to 4 tablespoonfuls cereal, vegetables or table scraps.

$\frac{1}{2}$ to 1 tablespoonful cod-liver oil twice a day.

Age 7 Months

Gradually eliminate noon meal.

Age 8 Months

Morning: $\frac{1}{4}$ to $\frac{1}{2}$ cup milk; $\frac{1}{2}$ to 1 slice buttered toast, or 1 to 2 tablespoonfuls cereal.

Evening: 2 to 5 heaping tablespoonfuls meat; 2 to 5 tablespoonfuls cereal, vegetables, or table scraps; $\frac{1}{2}$ to 1 slice buttered toast.

$\frac{1}{2}$ to 1 teaspoonful cod-liver oil twice a day.

Age 9 Months

The feeding for 8 months may be continued as mature diet, or the morning meal eliminated and the dog fed the 10 month's diet.

Age 10 Months—Mature

$\frac{1}{4}$ to $\frac{3}{4}$ cups meat

$\frac{1}{4}$ to $\frac{3}{4}$ cups cereal, or 1 to 2 slices buttered toast

$\frac{1}{4}$ to $\frac{3}{4}$ cups vegetables, or table scraps.

$\frac{1}{2}$ to 1 teaspoonful cod-liver oil twice a day, until warm weather.

Age 2 Months

Morning: 3 to 6 tablespoonfuls milk; 1½ to 3 tablespoonfuls cereal.

Noon: 2 to 4 heaping teaspoonfuls raw ground meat.

Afternoon: Repeat morning feeding.

Late evening: 3 to 6 tablespoonfuls milk.

½ to 1 teaspoonful cod-liver oil once a day.

Age 3 Months

Gradually increase amounts per feeding, according to puppy's growth and capacity. Gradually eliminate afternoon and late evening feeding.

Age 4 Months

Morning: ¼ to ½ cup milk; 2 to 4 tablespoonfuls cereal.

Noon: 2 to 4 heaping tablespoonfuls meat.

Evening: 2 to 4 tablespoonfuls cooked, mashed vegetables.

¼ to 1 teaspoonful cod-liver oil twice a day.

Age 5 Months

Increase amounts of food per meal.

Age 6 Months

Morning: ¾ to 1½ cups milk; ⅓ to ⅔ cups cereal.

Noon: 3 to 6 heaping tablespoonfuls meat; 3 to 6 tablespoonfuls cereal.

Evening: 4 to 8 heaping tablespoonfuls meat; 4 to 8 tablespoonfuls cereal, vegetables, or table scraps.

1 to 2 teaspoonfuls cod-liver oil twice a day.

Age 7 Months

Gradually eliminate noon meal.

Age 8 Months

Morning: ¾ to 1½ cups milk; 2 to 4 slices buttered toast, or 4 to 8 tablespoonfuls cereal.

Evening: ¾ to 2 cups meat; 3 to 5 slices toast, or 4 to 8 tablespoonfuls cereal; ½ to 1 cup vegetables, or table scraps.

1 to 2 teaspoonfuls cod-liver oil twice a day.

Age 9 Months

Begin to decrease amount of food as growing period is about over.

Age 10 Months

Morning: ½ to 1 cup milk; 1 to 2 slices buttered toast, or 2 to 4 tablespoonfuls cereal.

Evening: ¾ to 1½ cups meat; ½ to 1 cup cereal, or 2 to 4 slices toast; ½ to 1 cup vegetables, or table scraps.

1 to 2 teaspoonfuls cod-liver oil twice a day.

Age 11 Months

Continue as mature diet, or eliminate morning meal, and feed the 12 months' diet.

Age 12 Months

¾ to 1¼ cups meat; ¾ to 1¼ cups cereal, or 2 to 4 slices buttered toast; ¾ to 1¼ cups vegetables, or table scraps.

1 to 2 teaspoonfuls cod-liver oil, twice a day, until warm weather.

Age 2 Months

Morning: 5 to 6 tablespoonfuls milk; 3 to 4 tablespoonfuls cereal.

Noon: 1 to 2 heaping tablespoonfuls raw ground meat.

Afternoon: Repeat morning feeding.

Evening: Repeat noon feeding.

Late evening: 5 to 6 tablespoonfuls milk. 1 to 2 teaspoonfuls cod-liver oil twice a day.

Age 3 Months

Increase amounts per feeding—according to puppy's growth and capacity. Gradually eliminate afternoon and late evening feeding.

Age 4 Months

Morning: $\frac{1}{2}$ to 1 cup milk; 4 to 8 tablespoonfuls cereal.

Noon: 4 to 8 heaping tablespoonfuls meat.

Evening: 4 to 8 heaping tablespoonfuls meat; 3 to 6 tablespoonfuls cooked mashed vegetables.

3 to 5 teaspoonfuls cod-liver oil twice a day.

Age 5 Months

Increase amounts per feeding.

Age 6 Months

Morning: $\frac{3}{4}$ to $1\frac{1}{2}$ cups milk; $\frac{3}{4}$ to $1\frac{1}{2}$ cups cereal.

Noon: $\frac{1}{2}$ to 1 cup meat; $\frac{1}{2}$ to 1 cup cereal.

Evening: 1 to 2 cups meat; $\frac{1}{2}$ to 1 cup cereal; $\frac{1}{2}$ to 1 cup vegetables or table scraps.

$1\frac{1}{2}$ to 2 tablespoonfuls cod-liver oil twice a day, or vitamin concentrate.

Age 7 Months

Gradually eliminate noon meal for the 30-pound dog.

Age 8 Months (30 pounds)

Morning: $1\frac{1}{2}$ cups milk; 4 slices buttered toast, or 8 tablespoonfuls cereal.

Evening: 2 cups meat; 5 slices toast, or $\frac{1}{2}$ cup cereal; 1 cup vegetables, or table scraps.

$1\frac{1}{2}$ tablespoonfuls cod-liver oil twice a day, or vitamin concentrate.

Age 8 Months (45 pounds)

Morning: 2 cups milk; 2 cups cereal.

Noon: $1\frac{1}{2}$ cups meat; 1 cup cereal.

Evening: 2 cups meat; 1 cup cereal or toast; 1 cup vegetables, or table scraps.

$2\frac{1}{2}$ tablespoonfuls cod-liver oil or vitamin concentrate.

Age 9 Months

Gradually eliminate noon meal for 50-pound dog and start to reduce amount of food.

Age 10 Months

Morning: 1 to $1\frac{1}{2}$ cups milk; 2 to 3 slices toast, or $\frac{1}{2}$ to $\frac{3}{4}$ cups cereal.

Evening: $1\frac{1}{2}$ to $2\frac{1}{2}$ cups meat; 1 cup cereal, or 4 to 6 slices toast; 1 cup vegetables, or table scraps.

$1\frac{1}{2}$ to 3 tablespoonfuls cod-liver oil twice a day, or vitamin concentrate.

Age 11 Months

Continue 10 months' diet for 30-pound dog, or eliminate morning feeding. Further reduce amount of food for 50-pound dog, or eliminate morning meal.

Age 12 to 14 Months

$1\frac{1}{4}$ to $1\frac{3}{4}$ cups meat; $1\frac{1}{4}$ to $1\frac{3}{4}$ cups cereal or toast; $1\frac{1}{4}$ to $1\frac{3}{4}$ cups vegetables or table scraps.

$1\frac{1}{2}$ to 3 tablespoonfuls cod-liver oil and vitamin concentrate twice a day until warm weather.

There will be times when your Poodle will not want to eat at all. Like a human, he may simply not be hungry. Take his food away after about fifteen minutes. This may revive his appetite for the next meal. If he still misses a meal or two, think nothing of it, he will soon become hungry.

How often we forget that a dog's digestive system is, in some ways, more efficient than ours. Almost everything we can eat, he can eat too. On a road trip, don't hesitate to give him a hot dog or hamburger—no mustard or relish, though—and he'll enjoy eating it as much as you do.

Housebreaking

Housebreaking is helping your puppy to become a member of the family. Poodles naturally like to be clean and the sooner you provide a special place for yours the happier he will be. When placing newspapers in his enclosed area—and don't skimp—be affectionate, and tell him this spot belongs to him. Give him loving pats as a sign of your approval when he relieves himself upon the newspaper. If he starts to make a mistake, rush him to the newspaper to complete the job there.

After a few days begin to reduce the number of newspaper pages until you are down to one or two. The pup will soon get the idea that the single newspaper is his one and only spot. The odor of a slightly soiled newspaper will attract him. Commercial products are available with which to scent fresh newspaper as an indication of where he is to go.

Nature calls to a puppy after meals. If the weather is bad, let him use his place indoors, but if weather permits always take him outside. This applies, of course, to the very young pup. The older one should be taken out regardless of the weather. As soon as he has relieved himself outside, bring him back in immediately. Returning him home quickly will teach him the purpose of these trips.

Housebreaking your pup, if carried out with moderation, affection, and patience, achieves long-lasting results. Whenever you are training him remember that, like people, puppies need understanding—an attitude highly essential for later training.

Getting along with people

The essence of the word PET is ". . . getting along with people. . . ." If he is to be your friend and companion, your pet must learn his name. This can be accomplished during the housebreaking period. Select a short name for him and use it every time you address him. It should be distinctive and not sound like any other name in the household. He will quickly learn to recognize it. When he responds to it, reward him with a caress or a tidbit. In the early stage of all his training, call him by name frequently, and always reward him when he responds.

No question about it, your frisky and inquisitive pup will sometimes hop up on the furniture. From the beginning, you must make clear to him that your sofa, couch, table, etc., are off bounds. A sharp rebuke will soon teach him to keep away. When he is teething, you should not leave wallets, shoes, rubbers, and slippers carelessly around the house. Purchase a hard rubber bone or ball for him, a toy that he can call his own. In a short time, he will have lost his enthusiasm for chewing anything else.

Patient, attentive and loving

The key to Poodle training lies in your attitude. Both of you will have a pleasant time if you remain patient, attentive, loving and persistent in your efforts. Make him feel that his training has meaning. Such rewards as small tidbits of food, companionship, a satisfying grooming, will interest him in learning new things. The basis of all training may be summed up in these words: Don't give a command unless you can enforce it! Once you have given an order make sure that it is obeyed!

It requires a little time for a dog to get a clear idea of what you want him to accomplish. You must be prepared to repeat your commands until you are sure he understands. Praise him and reward him when he does well. Poodles are intelligent and anxious to learn.

4 Learning the obedience commands

Your Poodle should be taught the simple rules of obedience. They consist of the commands: "Come", "Sit", "Down", and "Heel". Outdoors your dog will naturally want to go off and play with other dogs or chase birds and cats. For his own safety and your peace of mind, he should be taught to walk close to you. How do you teach him this? Purchase a comfortable leash and collar for him. Let him sniff the collar. Then praise him lavishly as you put it on.

After he is used to it, take him out for a stroll. He may prefer to linger behind and will pull or plunge against the lead. After a few steps, stop and pull him to your left side while calling him by name. When he reaches you, praise and pet him until he quiets down. Then start off again, calling him as you go, until he learns to follow in the direction the leash tugs. He will soon discover that it is useless to struggle and more comfortable to walk along than be dragged. Each time he ceases to struggle, pet him and reward him. When he becomes frightened, reassure him. Soon he will learn to look forward to these strolls and to associate the leash with them.

To come

Learning to come when called by voice or whistle is next. Do not expect your pup to pick up this accomplishment immediately. Take him outside. Attach a light check cord at least twenty feet long to his collar. Allow him to have a short

SALLY ANNE THOMPSON
You may expect your puppy to pull at the beginning.

romp. When his attention has become attracted to something else, call him by name and give him the command "Come". When he responds, pat him, reward him, and allow him to continue his romp, calling him to you at intervals.

Soon he will become tired of having his pleasure interfered with and will refuse to come when ordered. Grasp the end of the check cord, repeat the command "Come", and give the cord a sharp jerk. He will probably try to resist, but keep repeating the command. A few sharp jerks will bring him to you. Reward him with a tidbit and caress. Repeat this several times before you end the lesson.

Never allow a lesson to go on too long. This training may be repeated several times a day, but having him come to you three or four times in each session is enough. Never, under any circumstances call your dog to you for punishment. If punishment or scolding is necessary, go to him. When you

"Sit". Push down with the left hand, pull back and up with the right and he will respond automatically.

call, he should always know that something pleasant is going to happen—if only a pat on the head.

To sit

With the dog standing in front of you or by your side, hold the leash in your right hand and give the command "Sit". At the same time lean over and with your left hand press down steadily on his rump until he is in a sitting position. Slip a tidbit in his mouth and praise him. Repeat this ritual several times, using the same command and pressing down on his rump. Soon he will associate the command with the pressure and anticipate it by sitting without being touched. You can then begin keeping him in a sitting position for longer periods of time.

"Down": After you have taught him to "Sit", it is not very difficult to teach him what "Down" means. Holding your pet by the collar with one hand, give the command "Down". Press on his rump with the other. When he is sitting, use the right hand to pull his front feet out from under him while you press down on his shoulder with the left hand and repeat the command "Down". Give the command "Up" when you allow him to rise. As you give the command take a few steps and he'll "Up" to follow you. Repetition of this practice will soon teach the dog to go down at the command "Down". You may raise your hand while you are voicing the command. Finally, all that is needed to cause the dog to drop down is to bring the hand into a raised position. The dog can be taught to remain "Down" for long periods if desired.

To "Heel"

This is the correct way to walk a mature dog. The loop of the leash is held in your right hand, the thong passes across your body to the dog who is on your left; control the slack of the leash with your left hand, shortening it or lengthening it as necessary.

Say clearly, "Rover, heel!" and start out with your left foot. When the dog strains ahead, jerk back sharply with your left hand but let the leash slacken instantly. Never pull the dog back into position; never drag him forward. It accomplishes nothing. The quick jerk is what does it. It makes him momentarily uncomfortable and he quickly learns that if he walks correctly at your left knee there will be no jerk. Keep walking, keep repeating "Heel", keep jerking when necessary. Remember to praise him when he walks properly. You'll be surprised how quickly he learns.

5   Good grooming

The bath: While dog experts argue pro and con whether dogs should be bathed regularly or not, the fact of the matter is that there are going to be times when your Poodle will need a bath. Make it no oftener than once a month unless there's an emergency—like his climbing out of a coal bin, for instance. Never give him a bath before he's six months old. You can use one of the commercially prepared aerosol foam baths to give a pup a dry cleaning. The foam is simply sprayed on and toweled off. These dry baths are particularly useful in winter. The bath water should be roughly the same as the dog's own temperature, about 101°F. It should be deep enough to touch his underbody when he stands upright in the tub. A rubber-hose portable spray will come in handy for wetting him down and rinsing him. Use a soap or shampoo designed for dogs, working the lather well down into the skin because that is where the real dirt is. Do not use any soap on his head. Merely wipe it and his muzzle and ears off with a damp washcloth, making very sure that no suds get into the eyes, ears, or nose. Overdo the rinsing to make sure you get out every bit of soap. Then after allowing him one vigorous shake wrap him up in an old towel and rub him vigorously to stimulate the circulation. A portable hair dryer can be used for the finishing touches, or he can be exercised indoors if it's cold out, outdoors if the weather is warm.

A deft touch

A Poodle owner accepts the responsibility of either grooming his pet at home or sending him to a beauty parlor. Grooming a Poodle requires practice and artistry. All experts agree that only professional Poodle trimmers can do a superlative job of trimming. One reason for such a claim is that show judges

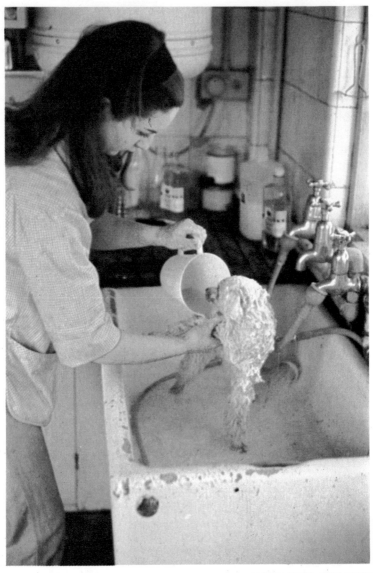

A little blueing in the rinse water will make his coat whiter.

Dry him thoroughly to avoid the risk of "colds".

accept only three types of clipping—all requiring an extremely deft touch. Most owners, however, prefer Poodle clips that are more simple.

If you have decided to groom your Poodle at home, you will need the following special grooming tools:

Clippers: with fine, medium, coarse and skip-tooth blades
Scissors: blunt and sharp
Rake
Nail Clippers
Tweezers
Wire Brush

Only the trial and error of experience can teach you how to use of clippers. Another book in this series, KNOW HOW TO CLIP A POODLE (No. 582), explains in great detail how to go about it. As for the blunt scissors, they are used to clip the hair around the Poodle's ears and face. The other pair of scissors has a sharp point used for cutting tiny hairs between the toes and for overall trimming. The rake is used to remove mats and tangles from his coat. The nail clippers must be used very carefully to avoid cutting a blood vessel. Use a stiff brush with long wire bristles. The tweezers are necessary to remove the hair from his ears.

Styles of simple clipping

A simple clip for beginners is the Lamb clip. The Poodle is clipped close on the body and neck. The legs are trimmed moderately full. Both the tail pompon and the top knot are well defined. The Lamb clip is very attractive and can be easily altered to correct any mistakes a beginner might make.

The most popular clip in America is the Dutch. The stately top knot, tail pompon and partially full body make this a particularly distinguished style. The legs are full. The feet are clipped clean around the dewclaw mark. One stripe follows the spine and another which should reach forward on the underside, runs about his midsection. There are a considerable number of variations of this clip of which the Royal Dutch is the easiest to maintain.

The Riviera Clip is highly elegant and somewhat similar to the Continental Clip. Its main characteristics are leg bracelets and a closely shaved rear. There are other attractive clips which bear such exotic names as the Palm Springs, the Las Vegas and the Kerry. These are often used by Poodle fanciers who have no intention of entering their dogs for show.

Clip the nails gingerly

Watching your Poodle romping in the open on wide grassy spaces, giving vent to all his energy, exercising his freedom to his heart's content is a joyful sight to behold. However, no matter how much you let him romp, if he does not get the chance to exercise on concrete or gravel, his nails will need attention.

Try to make his clipping as quick and pleasant as possible. Keep him absolutely still to eliminate the danger of nipping a blood vessel. Every time you bring your pet to the veterinarian, he will, if you wish, clip the nails. While you're there, ask him for some tips on clipping. To reduce the number of clippings you should file the points of his nails every two or three weeks with a flat wood-file. The file should be drawn in only one direction from the top of the nail downward in a round stroke to the end of the nail or underneath. Considerable pressure is needed for a few strokes in order to get through the hard polished surface of the nail.

6 General care

Dogs are very much like people in many respects. While proper food, shelter, exercise and sanitation are all very

Clip the foot in its entirety, on top, underneath and between the toes.

Loose hairs and ragged edges are smoothed down with a scissors.

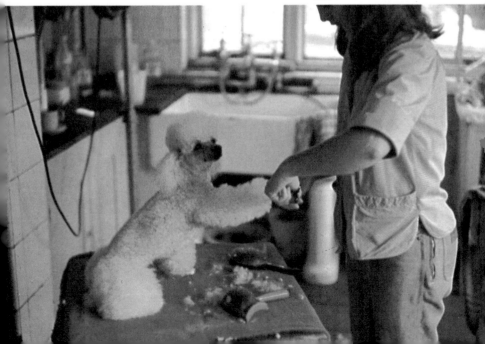

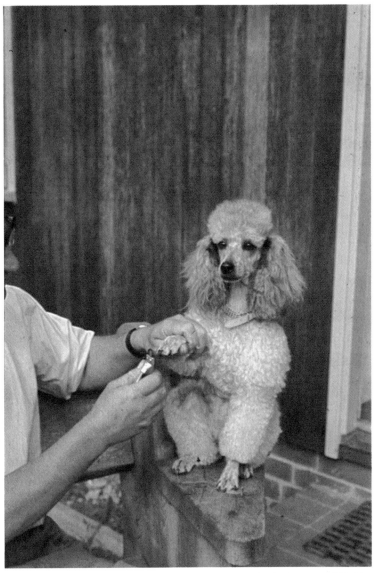

Hold the nails against the light. The dark area in the center is the quick. Avoid cutting into it.

essential to the health and good temperament of a dog, attention, companionship and affection also play an important part in his well-being. Poodles are hardy individuals, able to adapt themselves to almost any living conditions. Pampering is unnecessary and should for the dog's own sake be avoided. This does not mean, however, that he is not entitled to the attention of his master.

Every dog owner should spend at least a little time every day with his pet, in addition to looking after his necessities. Of course, if the dog is kept in the house, he sees much of the family and becomes part of it. But if he is kept in a kennel, he should be removed from his confines at least once daily, given a period of exercise on a leash and if possible, a good romp in an open space where he is not likely to get into mischief. These periods can be employed to train your Poodle in the niceties of behavior. They allow time for a good brisk grooming so essential to the development and maintenance of a good healthy coat and skin.

First aid

Most of the time your Poodle is able to take care of himself. Generally, he will lick a small cut or wound and it will heal. However, you may treat such small wounds as you would your own. Thoroughly clean the wound and apply a mild antiseptic or first aid cream.

However, he cannot remove a thorn from his paw, or a burr from his coat, nor can he set a broken leg. Remember, if your dog is hurt, he will be looking to you for help. Don't become overly excited. Carefully examine him before you move him. If he has a broken bone you must apply a splint before moving him. Keeping the leg as straight as possible, attach a splint to the leg by tying it above and below the break.

Nearly all dogs hurt in accidents suffer from shock. The heart beats faster but weaker and they often seem oblivious to pain. Shock needs treatment before any minor cuts or breaks are given attention. It is best treated by covering the dog with a warm blanket and keeping him warm. If he can swallow, the simplest household stimulant to administer is coffee with sugar and cream and a pinch of salt. Gently lift his head, loosen the muzzle and pour the coffee into a pocket made by pulling out his lip.

After any treatment, notify the veterinarian. If he thinks you can handle it he will tell you so.

Cuts

The feet of dogs have numerous small blood vessels which can bleed profusely from even a small cut. Should the cut be severe, or the blood flow difficult to staunch, you may wish to apply a tourniquet between the cut and the heart. Relax the pressure for a few seconds every five or ten minutes. A normal cut needs only a pressure bandage. This should be firmly applied to help create a blood clot. Should the bandage be applied too loosely, it will merely sponge up blood rather than prevent the flow. Leave this bandage on until a clot seems to have formed.

It may be necessary for the veterinarian to suture the cut. This will help the wound heal and can have your Poodle as active as ever in ten days or less. Just make sure a clean bandage is applied every second day.

Accidental poisoning and antidotes

Poisoned animals require immediate attention. Administer first aid measures before rushing him to the vet's. If you know the poison, apply the antidote listed on the label of the container or consult the accompanying chart. However if you are not sure, use the following general procedure.

Empty his stomach by giving him a 3% solution of hydrogen peroxide mixed half-and-half with water. A tablespoon for each ten pounds of dog is required. This turns into oxygen and water inside his stomach, causing him to vomit, but is

otherwise harmless. It takes about two minutes to act. Let his stomach settle and then give him some Epsom salts, a teaspoonful in some water to empty his bowels quickly.

The hydrogen peroxide is an antidote for phosphorus, while Epsom salts are proper medication against lead poisoning. A third antidote that can be given that is effective against two other poisons is the "hypo" used in photographic darkrooms. A teaspoonful in water is sufficient.

However, try to determine the poison and apply proper rather than expedient antidotes.

Household antidotes for common poisons

Poison	Antidote (for 40-lb dog)
Mercuric compounds	Egg white, milk, half a cup
Arsenic	Sodium thiosulphate (ordinary photographer's "hypo"), 1 teaspoonful in water
Acids	Bicarbonate of soda, eggshells, crushed plaster, 1 tablespoonful
Alkalis	Vinegar, lemon juice, several tablespoonsful
Lead	Epsom salts, 1 teaspoonful in water
Phosphorus	Peroxide of hydrogen, as directed for emetic
Thallium	Table salt, 1 teaspoonful in water
Strychnine	Sedative drugs (nembutal, phenobarbital), 1 grain to each 7 lb of weight
Sedative drugs	Strong coffee, 1 cupful
Food poisoning	Peroxide of hydrogen, empty bowels with enema of warm water, when stomach has settled give Epsom salts, 1 teaspoonful in water

7   Common ailments

As do people, dogs have their ups and downs. But a dog who has had a proper series of inoculations, a steady and nourishing diet, plenty of exercise, has had clean quarters and a daily brushing is likely to remain a healthy dog. When concerned about your dog's health, a good axiom to keep in mind is, "An ounce of prevention is worth a pound of cure". Knowing the symptoms of common diseases will enable you to spot them immediately and to give the veterinarian a general idea of what is wrong. Following is a list of common ailments.

Diarrhea

This is a common ailment. A change of diet, excitement and improper feeding are the usual causes. Give your dog Kaopectate, or milk of bismuth. A teaspoonful to a tablespoon every three hours, the quantity depends on the size of your dog. If his condition persists, consult your veterinarian.

Constipation

A diet of rich and starchy foods may harden in the bowels. Your dog needs plenty of roughage, exercise and ample opportunity for relieving himself. These simple measures can usually solve the worst constipation problem. But if it persists, use milk of magnesia or mineral oil. It there are no results call your veterinarian.

Distemper

True distemper, which is correctly called Carre's disease after the man who studied it, is seldom seen today thanks to our advanced methods of immunization. However, the word distemper is frequently used in a generic sense to indicate a

A good appetite denotes a healthy puppy.

dog with a generalized set of symptoms. Used in this way the prognosis might vary from good to fair to poor, depending on what is actually causing the symptoms.

There are a number of problems occurring in puppies the symptoms of which, particularly in their early stages, are very similar, and accurate diagnosis is almost impossible. These symptoms include elevated temperature, mucousy nose and/or eyes, loss of appetite, diarrhea, listlessness, frequent productive sneezing, vomiting and a deep cough, low in the abdomen, as distinguished from a bronchial cough which is in the upper region.

These symptoms alone are sufficient to suspect distemper although, by themselves, they do not support a positive diagnosis as many other, less serious diseases will frequently cause the same symptoms.

Additional symptoms more characteristic of true distemper are photophobia, or fear of light, a distinctive temperature curve and conjunctivitis. The puppy will hide in dimly lit areas and, when exposed to light, will squint and show his discomfort. Another distinctive symptom is the so-called diphasic, or saddle, curve of temperature. From the normal of 101 to 102.2°F. the puppy's temperature will shoot up as high as 105°F. on the fifth day after infection, followed by a drop to almost normal on the sixth. This is followed by a rise to 103 or 104°F. and it remains approximately that for the duration of the disease.

Conjunctivitis is an inflammation of the conjunctiva, the membranes lining the eyelids.

Frequently, sores are seen on the stomach. The skin, when pinched, retains the crease, returning slowly to normal in contrast to the skin of a healthy dog which snaps back.

In the early stages keep the puppy warm and check its temperature daily keeping a written record. This will help your veterinarian make a positive diagnosis should the symptoms persist. Baby aspirins can be given three or four times daily and the puppy should be hand-fed if necessary. Boil 4 oz of milk and 4 oz of water and allow them to cool. Add 2 oz of Karo syrup, the yolk of an egg and a pinch of salt and mix well. Give it to the puppy freely. Should you have to resort to spoon-feeding, pull out the lips at the side to form a pocket and pour in a spoonful at a time. Allow ample time for it to go down before giving another. Make sure he gets nourishment often.

Simple diarrhea can be controlled by administering Kaopectate or milk of bismuth. For small puppies, give one tablespoon initially, followed by one teaspoon every three hours, or after every movement. For larger dogs increase the dosage in proportion to his size.

Should symptoms persist you must, of course, contact your veterinarian. However, do not become unduly discouraged. While distemper, when it does appear, is extremely serious, antibiotics help control the secondary infection and with good nursing there is a decent percentage of cures. Some, but by no means all, puppies are left with aftereffects which might range from hardly noticeable to severe, but many do make a complete recovery. Should it turn out that it wasn't true distemper after all, but one of the other puppy ailments, chances are good for a complete recovery.

Vaccination

Today the science of immunization has developed to a remarkable degree. Puppies can be given a long-lasting immunity to distemper by the time that they are ten weeks old. Your veterinarian can also inoculate your puppy with antibodies which, while their effect is measured in days, will serve to protect him until he can receive his permanent inoculation. At the same time that he is giving the distemper shots, your veterinarian may also immunize your puppy against hepatitis and leptospirosis. We will not go into a description of these diseases here as, in the early stages, their symptoms are similar to those described for distemper. An accurate diagnosis had best be left to your veterinarian who is trained to differentiate.

Be safe—have your puppy immunized before any symptoms appear as the value of inoculation, once he has contracted the disease, is doubtful.

Tracheobronchitis

"Kennel Cough", or tracheobronchitis is a mild ailment affecting puppies. They appear to be attempting to clear their throat and produce a gagging cough that is usually most severe during the night. Otherwise, the pup appears normal and both his appetite and bowel movements are as they should be. Eyes and nose are clear and his temperature ranges between 101 and 102.2°F. which is normal. "Kennel Cough", though not serious, is a highly contagious illness that is prevalent where puppies are kept in crowded quarters.

Luckily, "Kennel Cough" is a self-limiting disease. Pups usually recover without medication although they may have their rasping cough for as long as forty days. Nevertheless, cough mixtures may help alleviate the symptoms and these can be purchased at pet counters. Should the cough be severe or last an abnormal length of time, your veterinarian can prescribe sulfa drugs or one of the antibiotics (such as chloromycetin).

Tooth disorders

Your Poodle should be allowed to gnaw large bones, hard rubber toys and rawhide bones to keep his teeth strong and clean. Where discoloration shows, wipe the teeth with hydrogen peroxide and a piece of cloth. Toothpaste mixed with powdered pumice can also be used.

Eye care

The eyes should be watched carefully. After each romp into high grass or cover, weed seeds and foreign matter should be flushed out with warm water, because the presence of such

Examine your dog's teeth regularly. SALLY ANNE THOMPSON

material is exceedingly irritating and may cause serious damage. A commercially prepared eyewash can be found at most pet counters for general care of the eyes.

Common cold

The symptoms of the cold are similar in dog and human, although your pet is likely to suffer from loose bowels. Kao-pectate will take care of this. Terramycin works wonders with dog's colds: as this drug is available only on prescription you must ask your veterinarian for it.

In the last fifteen years veterinary science has improved to such a degree that most of the major dog diseases can be cared for successfully.

Never probe deeper than you can see.

Ear canker

The Poodle that paws and scratches his ears occasionally might have an ear infection, or might be scratching for the joy of scratching. Persistent scratching calls for a careful inspection. Check the ears for a brown, waxy substance that is a sign of ear canker. If not corrected promptly, it might become troublesome. Take a cotton swab, dip it in olive oil and remove as much of this secretion as possible. A commercially prepared medicated ear wash, available in most pet departments, is quite effective when used as directed.

Worms and worming

Even the best-cared-for dogs sometimes get worms. But not all worms are the same. There are roundworms, hookworms, whipworms, and tapeworms, just to name a few. Each requires its own special treatment. So be sure of your worm and the medication you're using if you decide to worm the animal yourself. Symptoms: Actual appearance of the worm or segments of it in stools and vomit. A "potbelly", diarrhea, persistent vomiting, runny eyes and nose.

Roundworms: These worms, common in puppies, are fortunately fairly easy to get rid of. They are quite long, white or pinkish, and tend to coil up like watchsprings— hence their name. Easily used and effective medication for roundworms will be found at the pet shop.

If you are not sure of the kind of worm which is infecting your dog, take a sample of his stool to the vet's for micro- scopic examination, and then let him prescribe the treatment.

Fleas

This problem must be attacked on two fronts. You have not only to rid your dog of the fleas and eggs infesting his body, you must also exterminate the eggs which have dropped off in those areas where he moves and sleeps. Use a good com- mercial flea powder or aerosol spray, following the directions on the container. Then completely disinfect his quarters and bed. This done, go over the dog with a brush and fine comb, getting rid of all the dead or dying parasites. Never neglect a dog's fleas or ticks. They are the cause of serious skin problems.

8   Poodle breeding

To the real dog-lover, there is no happier sight than that of a healthy and contented mother with an attractive litter of Poodle puppies. Your joy is even greater when you know these are the offspring of your own beloved pet. Your participation in the daily life and growth of a happy litter of Poodle puppies will be sure to fascinate you.

If you already have a female, let nature assert herself at least once or twice during your female's lifetime. Giving birth and rearing a litter is the natural fulfillment of her life. After having successfully completed her motherly chores, she will become more mature in many ways; healthier, more obedient and loyal.

Non-professional breeding of Poodles with the sole object of making money is usually disappointing. Breed your female for the sheer pleasure of the pastime accepting any profit as an additional piece of luck.

Once you have decided to breed a litter you may be fortunate enough to obtain the services of a friend's Poodle or one of your neighbor's pets. If not, you will have to make arrangements with a professional breeder. The cost of his stud fee ranges from $50 to $250. Before mating, you must make sure your female has booster shots, worming checks and an excellent diet with a full complement of vitamins. If your dog is of exceptionally fine quality you should carefully check a stud's background to see how consistently he has won on the bench.

It was once common procedure to let the stud's owner have the pick of the litter instead of a cash fee. This is never a wise practice. You are paying more for the service than it is worth by losing the most active puppy of the litter. If you are breeding Toys, who often have only one or two puppies, you may finish empty-handed. It is common practice for your agreement to provide a repeat mating at no charge should the first one fail to "take".

Your female will carry her young for about nine weeks. There are many warning signs to indicate that the moment is near. She will often seem restless and may decide to sleep in a new and strange place. She will aimlessly scratch at her bedding and become pre-occupied with licking or biting herself. A drop in temperature is a sure indication that birth

Standard Poodle Ch. Puttencove Privateer.

is near. Give your veterinarian due warning and then let nature take its course, trying not to upset your mother-to-be.

A Standard's normal litter is approximately six to eight puppies.

A Miniature Poodle's normal litter is about three to five, although they may have as few as one or as many as eleven. For the first few days after giving birth, your female should be kept on a light diet of easily digestible foods, such as milk, cheese and broth. On the second or third day you may include some boiled fish, followed with a diet of boiled meats and

The look of intelligence.

possibly cooked eggs, until the end of the week when she is back on her normal schedule.

Between the third and sixth day your puppies should have their tails docked and their dewclaws removed. At this age they are too young to feel anything but minimal discomfort and healing is rapid. You will save yourself and the mother unnecessary anxiety by keeping her away from the scene of this minor operation.

Remember that your Poodles are happiest when they are with you. It may be difficult to have all your Poodles in the house with you at the same time. Why not alternate them—keeping one in your house while the others remain in the kennel. This will keep your dogs happy and it will show them that you love all of them equally.

Choose your puppies' new home with care!!

9 Scientific breeding

Thanks to the pioneering studies of heredity by the nine-teenth-century Monk, Gregory Mendel, the breeding of dogs has become a science. Without his "Law of Alternate Inheritance" the incredible advance in our knowledge of heredity in the last fifty years would have been impossible. Mendel's work described the inheritance of certain traits in plants as possessing a dominant and recessive relationship. The application of Mendel's Law to dogs is easily demonstrated by the following example:

A breeder mates a pure black Poodle to a white Poodle. As white is a recessive color we know that it cannot conceal black which is dominant. A friend has made the same kind of mating. All the puppies will be black, but they will be carrying genes for white. They each raise the pups to adulthood. Then they decide to mate a pup from one litter with a pup from the other. The pups from this mating should be

75% black and 25% white. Of the blacks, one third of them will be pure black while the others will be carrying genes for white.

The puppies from this cross of two hybrids may actually be all of one color or the other or even a different proportion than we expected. But our case doesn't contradict Mendel's Law. It simply shows there weren't enough pups for the mathematical expectancy to be realized. It is just as if we took a black and a white marble which one parent contributed and dropped them in a hat; then took two more which the other parent contributed. You'd have two black and two white marbles. Reach into the hat now and take out two. Record the color. Put them back, mix them and take out two more. Keep doing it and record what you had each time until you have drawn out 100 pairs. You will find you have very close to 25 times drawn a pair of white, 25 times drawn a pair of black and 50 times a pair composed of one black and one white. Now you might draw a pair of black several times in a row, but the great average is 25-50-25.

Thus, in any one litter the exact expectancy is not always realized, but there is an expectancy, nonetheless. It is governed by the "Law of Alternate Inheritance". This question of skipping a generation is now, as we have seen, mathematically explainable.

10   Grooming for the bench

Once your Poodle has been entered for the show, the next step is to groom him according to the established rules. The uninitiated may look with some misgiving upon the first poodle they see with full-bloom coat clipped in the height of fashion. This is a long-time Poodle practice which is neither a fad nor impractical. It has certainly enhanced the dog's looks, and in no way has affected his character or abilities.

Learning to "Pose" for a show.

SALLY ANNE THOMPSON

Now, isn't he a lamb?

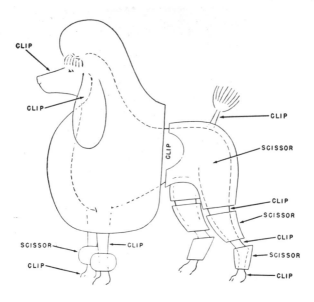

The chart depicts the English Saddle Clip. In the Continental Clip the scissored saddle is clipped bare except for rosettes on the hips.

The Feet

Clip the foot in its entirety, on top, underneath and between the toes. Start the lower bracelet about an inch above the toes.

The First Bracelet

At a point just above the hock, clip a band completely around the leg of an inch or two in width. In deciding on the width, be guided by the size of the dog and your own personal preference. This band or line must be parallel to the lower band above the toes and at a right angle with the leg. This completes the first bracelet and forms the lower line for the second bracelet.

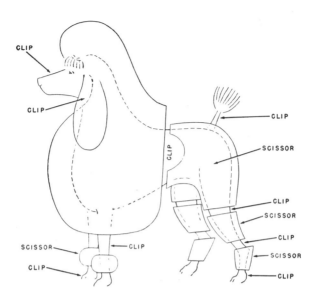

The Second Bracelet

This should extend to the first thigh joint. The upper and lower lines must be parallel. Be sure to clip the inside of the leg.

The Rear Coat

With the bracelets finished, the lower line of the saddle or "pants" has been formed. This should extend about an inch or an inch and a half below the crotch. Before the saddle is blocked out, the remaining rear coat should be cut with scissors to about one inch in length, trimming forward to the second or third from rear. If the dog has a long back, leave more ruff.

The Saddle

Begin the saddle point at the center of the spine, about an

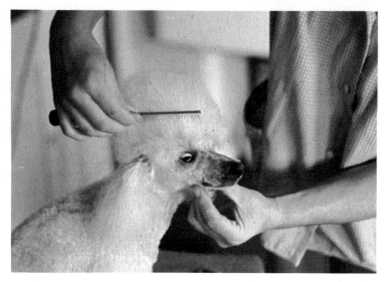

Comb the top knot up into a crown.

Now round it carefully with a scissors.

SALLY ANNE THOMPSON

inch back of the ruff. In clipping, follow the illustration, going back and downward. Miss the hip bone by about an inch. Move forward and downward toward the brisket to a point just back of the ruff. tapering as you go. Square this sharply, clipping a band parallel with the point at the center of the back, making it about an inch in width. Clip the other side the same way, making sure your design is correct.

It will be necessary to square off the lower edge of the "pants" with the scissors. Use the scissors on the saddle to get the hair to about three-fourths of an inch in length. The under part of the dog, back of the ruff, is clipped bare.

The Tail

The tail should be clipped from its base so that a pompon about three inches in length remains at the tip. Round off the pompon.

The Front Puffs

These should consist of a strip of coat about three inches wide. They should start about an inch above the toes. The legs should be clipped close above the puff.

The Head

Clip away from the eyes, not towards them. Clip out the end of the muzzle from the inner corner of the eye. Clean the cheeks well, clipping all intervening space. Clip an arc downward from the base of the ear to the center of the neck, about four or five inches below the lower jaw. Be sure to get both sides even. Clip under the jaw and the part of the throat desired.

The Finish

The finishing touches add much to the neatness of the job.

The bracelets and puffs should be scissored to about two inches in length. With comb and scissors square them where they appear to need it, so that they follow the natural lines of the leg structure. It will also be necessary to square off the lower edge of the "pants" with the scissors. Use the scissors on the saddle to get the hair to about three-fourths of an inch in length. The under part of the dog, back of the ruff, is clipped bare. It is in the finishing touches that the artistry of the trimmer is evidenced.

The Puppy Clip

The only acceptable show clip for puppies requires little grooming. A puppy's hair is too delicate for any pattern. A clipped face, feet, tail, stomach, and hair slightly trimmed to give a neat appearance, typify the Puppy Clip.

11   Pals with the Poodle

As your Poodle becomes older and more mature, you and he can become true companions. The Poodle is capable of a loyalty unique among dogs. His intelligence is humanlike in many ways. Poodle fanciers say that their pets always seem to know in advance what the human wants to do next. The next time you see a person walking with his Poodle, notice how the two are attuned to each other. A friendship so deep, so profound develops between master and pet, that only the word "affinity" can do justice to it.

Poodles are the embodiment of perkiness; they are the essence of "dogs". Ever see a Poodle at a picnic? They romp around for hours and when thrown a ball they retrieve with a truly professional style. Never miss watching a Poodle the first time he bounces into water. The grace with which he

SALLY ANNE THOMPSON
"Shaking Hands" comes naturally. This dog seems to be a lefty.

shakes off the water after he finishes his swim, confirms his position as Prince of the Canine Kingdom.

His natural playfulness will make it easy for you to teach your pet a few mutually entertaining tricks. To teach him to shake hands, have him sit and give the command "Shake" clearly while lifting his right paw and shaking it. Immediately reward him with a piece of dog candy. Repeat this several times a day. Within a week he will greet you in the morning with a raised paw.

Teaching him to beg is done in a similar manner. Command him to sit and lift his paws to the begging position. Repetition will enable him to learn his trick within a few weeks.

Poodles are very agile. It's a simple matter to teach them to "Beg". All that's needed is a little encouragement and a tidbit.

Poodles love to retrieve. Buy a hard rubber ball or bone at a reputable pet shop. Your dog can carry such toys safely in his mouth. If he doesn't immediately respond when you throw the ball, take him to the spot where the toy landed and return with it to your original position. Once he catches on, you can increase the distance you throw. Retrieving is a good way of exercising him and in getting to be pals with him.

Children and Poodles get along remarkably well together and will probably invent games of their own to play. The outdoor air seems fresher, the sunshine healthier, when a little boy or girl has a Poodle to go out and play with. A Poodle has that extra sense of humor that makes him appeal to all people, young and old, from every land.

THE PET LIBRARY LTD

The more information and knowledge you have about your pets, the more you will enjoy them. In the KNOW (64 pages) and ENJOY (32 pages) books, THE PET LIBRARY has created a complete series to help you take better care of your pets and get more pleasure from them. Both series are printed with living full-color pictures completely illustrating entire text.

DOGS

KNOW YOUR BASSET HOUND	501
KNOW YOUR BEAGLE	502
KNOW YOUR BOSTON TERRIER	503
KNOW YOUR BOXER	504
KNOW YOUR BULLDOG	505
KNOW YOUR CHIHUAHUA	506
KNOW YOUR COCKER SPANIEL	507
KNOW YOUR COLLIE	508
KNOW YOUR DACHSHUND	509
KNOW YOUR DALMATIAN	510
KNOW YOUR DOBERMAN PINSCHER	511
KNOW YOUR FOX TERRIER	512
KNOW YOUR GERMAN SHEPHERD	513
KNOW YOUR GREAT DANE	514
KNOW YOUR IRISH SETTER	515
KNOW YOUR MALTESE	516
KNOW YOUR MINIATURE SCHNAUZER	517
KNOW YOUR PEKINGESE	518
KNOW YOUR POMERANIAN	519
KNOW YOUR POODLE	520
KNOW YOUR PUG	521
KNOW YOUR RETRIEVER	522
KNOW YOUR SCOTTISH TERRIER	523
KNOW YOUR SHETLAND SHEEPDOG	524
KNOW YOUR WEIMARANER	525
KNOW YOUR YORKSHIRE TERRIER	526
KNOW YOUR LOVABLE MUTT	527

GENERAL DOG BOOKS

KNOW HOW TO CHOOSE YOUR DOG	581
KNOW HOW TO CLIP A POODLE	582
KNOW HOW TO GROOM YOUR DOG	583
KNOW FIRST AID FOR DOGS	584
KNOW HOW TO TRAIN YOUR GUARD DOG	585
KNOW HOW TO TRAIN YOUR PUPPY	586

CATS

KNOW YOUR DOMESTIC AND EXOTIC CATS	602
KNOW YOUR PERSIAN CAT	604
KNOW YOUR SIAMESE CAT	605

BIRDS

KNOW THE POPULAR CAGE BIRDS	651
KNOW YOUR CANARY	652
KNOW YOUR PARAKEET	656
KNOW YOUR PARROT	657
KNOW YOUR WILD BIRDS	659

FISHES

KNOW YOUR AQUARIUM	702
KNOW HOW TO BREED TROPICAL FISH	704
KNOW HOW TO BREED EGGLAYERS	705
KNOW YOUR GOLDFISH	711
KNOW YOUR GUPPIES	714
KNOW HOW TO KEEP SALT WATER FISHES	720

OTHER PET TITLES

KNOW YOUR HAMSTER	754
KNOW YOUR MONKEY	755
KNOW YOUR OCELOTS AND MARGAYS	756

DOGS

ENJOY YOUR BASSET HOUND 101
ENJOY YOUR BEAGLE 102
ENJOY YOUR BOSTON TERRIER 103
ENJOY YOUR BOXER 104
ENJOY YOUR CHIHUAHUA 106
ENJOY YOUR COCKER SPANIEL 107
ENJOY YOUR COLLIE 108
ENJOY YOUR DACHSHUND 109
ENJOY YOUR FOX TERRIER 112
ENJOY YOUR GERMAN SHEPHERD 113
ENJOY YOUR MINIATURE SCHNAUZER 117
ENJOY YOUR PEKINGESE 118
ENJOY YOUR POMERANIAN 119
ENJOY YOUR POODLE 120
ENJOY YOUR SCOTTISH TERRIER 123
ENJOY YOUR PUPPY 127

GENERAL DOG BOOKS

ENJOY YOUR DOG PICTURE BOOK 181
ENJOY TRAINING YOUR DOG 185

CATS

ENJOY CARING FOR YOUR CAT 201
ENJOY CARING FOR YOUR KITTEN 203
ENJOY YOUR PERSIAN CAT 204
ENJOY YOUR SIAMESE CAT 205

BIRDS

ENJOY YOUR CANARY 252
ENJOY YOUR COCKATIEL 253
ENJOY YOUR FINCHES 254
ENJOY YOUR MYNAH BIRD 255
ENJOY YOUR PARAKEET 256
ENJOY YOUR PARROT 257
ENJOY YOUR PIGEONS 258

FISHES

ENJOY YOUR ANGELFISH 301
ENJOY YOUR AQUARIUM 302
ENJOY YOUR BARBS 303
ENJOY BREEDING LIVEBEARERS 306
ENJOY YOUR CATFISH 307
ENJOY YOUR CICHLIDS 308
ENJOY YOUR DISCUS 309
ENJOY THE FIGHTING FISH FROM SIAM 310
ENJOY YOUR GOLDFISH 311
ENJOY YOUR GOURAMIS AND OTHER ANABANTIDS 312
ENJOY YOUR FANCY GUPPIES 313
ENJOY YOUR GUPPIES 314
ENJOY YOUR KILLIFISH 315
ENJOY YOUR MOLLIES 316
ENJOY PLANTING YOUR AQUARIUM 317
ENJOY YOUR PLATYS AND SWORDTAILS 318
ENJOY A SALT WATER AQUARIUM 319
ENJOY YOUR TETRAS 321
PREVENTION AND CARE—TROPICAL FISH DISEASES 322
ENJOY YOUR TROPICAL FISH PICTURE BOOK 323

OTHER PETS

ENJOY YOUR ALLIGATOR 351
ENJOY YOUR CHAMELEON 352
ENJOY YOUR GUINEA PIG 353
ENJOY YOUR HAMSTER 354
ENJOY YOUR MONKEY 355
ENJOY YOUR RABBIT 357
ENJOY YOUR RATS, MICE AND GERBILS 358
ENJOY YOUR SKUNK 359
ENJOY YOUR SNAKES 360
ENJOY YOUR TERRARIUM 361
ENJOY YOUR TURTLE 362

Publisher's suggested Retail:– ENJOY series (32 pages) 39c
KNOW series (64 pages) $1.00
(Retail prices may vary by geographical location and are subject to change without notice.)